ALSO BY JON DAVIS

BOOKS

Above the Bejeweled City
An Amiable Reception for the Acrobat
Improbable Creatures
Heteronymy: An Anthology
Preliminary Report
Scrimmage of Appetite
Dangerous Amusements

CHAPBOOKS

Loving Horses
Thelonious Sphere
Local Color
The Hawk. The Road. The Sunlight After Clouds.
West of New England

TRANSLATIONS

Dayplaces, by Naseer Hassan

CHOOSE YOUR OWN AMERICA

Jon Davis

Finishing Line Press
Georgetown, Kentucky

CHOOSE YOUR OWN AMERICA

"I'm writing for the ages. It'd be good if we had some."
—Chuck Calabreze

Copyright © 2022 by Jon Davis
ISBN 978-1-64662-924-4 First Edition
All rights reserved under International and Pan-American Copyright Conventions. No part of this book may be reproduced in any manner whatsoever without written permission from the publisher, except in the case of brief quotations embodied in critical articles and reviews.

ACKNOWLEDGMENTS

I thank the editors of the following journals for publishing these poems:

"Abjection," *Frank* (France)
"Apocalypse," *The Laurel Review*
"The Billville Electrocution," *Salt Hill*
"Choose Your Own America," *The Philadelphia Review of Books*
"Fashion Report," *The Laurel Review*
"The Failed Spring," *Terrain.org*
"Jane Says," *Hinchas de Poesia*
"Manatees," *Poetry at Sangam* (India)
"Militia," *Flash: The International Short-Short Story*
"Music Men," *McSweeney's Internet Tendency*
"Ode to the Coronavirus," *terrain.org*
"Popstar," *Versal*

"A Structure for Our Grief" appeared in *Poetry is Bread* (Nirala Publications, 2022).
"Ode to the Coronavirus," "Choose Your Own America," "Vintage," and "Above the Bejeweled City" appeared in *Four Quartets: Poetry in the Pandemic* (Tupelo Press, 2020).
"Theoretically," appeared in *Funny Bone: Flashing for Comic Relief* (The International Short-Short Story Press, 2017).
"Music Men," appeared in *Flash Fiction Funny* (Blue Light Press, 2013).

Some of these poems appeared in *An Amiable Reception for the Acrobat* (Grid Books, 2019) or *Above the Bejeweled City* (Grid Books, 2021).

With thanks to the Lannan Foundation and the Artists' Retreat at Cill Rialaig, County Kerry, Ireland, for the gift of time and solitude.

Publisher: Leah Huete de Maines
Editor: Christen Kincaid
Cover Art: Sherwin Bitsui
Author Photo: Jason Ordaz
Cover Design: Elizabeth Maines McCleavy

Order online: www.finishinglinepress.com
also available on amazon.com

Author inquiries and mail orders:
Finishing Line Press
PO Box 1626
Georgetown, Kentucky 40324
USA

Table of Contents

Choose Your Own America 1

Militia, 1960 2

Arran 3

Fashion Report 6

Popstar 7

Wish for a Young Wife 9

Petting Zoo, Cerrillos, New Mexico 10

Jane Says 11

Theoretically 13

Music Men 14

The Billville Execution 16

Carnal in the Land of Blood and Beauty 18

Abjection 19

The Failed Spring 21

Manatees 22

Apocalypse 23

The Room 24

Vintage 26

Ode to the Coronavirus 27

Above the Bejeweled City 28

The City of New Orleans 30

The Famous Poet 32

A Structure for Our Grief 34

Asterisk as Ornament 35

CHOOSE YOUR OWN AMERICA

You can choose the forefathered one,
all beard and stovepipe, folderol
and feather, all foppish at the brothel.
Or that earlier one, all lunge and gallop,
musket and scatter, belfry and blunderbuss.
Or the gangrenous and stooped one, caterwauling
on the White House lawn. You can choose
the haunted one, nightshakes, the guilt-worn
and riddled, still moaning in the willows.
Or the exuberant one, the one that prances—
gray squirrel on an electrical wire,
all pomp and reflex, tail toss and brass.
Then there's the worried one, furtive
in the hovel, the duckers and shamblers,
scriveners of the mud's cursive. Or the America
of duplicates and editions, of ranch houses
and khakis, quick pledge and the concrete walkway.
You can choose the America of granite,
of cobblestone, of quick strike and vanish.
Or the America of *gracias* in the market,
miigwech on the subway, never mind
the sleek traders on the balcony, the champagne
they drizzle on the occupying hordes below.

MILITIA, 1960

Jake said the meadow was filled with men with guns so we had to go look.

It was almost dark, August and still hot, the sun already down among the red maples and swamp oaks.

When we crawled over the hilltop to the edge of the woods, we could see twenty or thirty grown men in camo, hunkered at the edge of the field, up at the house end, by the abandoned chicken-house foundation. While we watched, they made a long line. One man pulled his cap off, wiping sweat and dust from his forehead. Someone signaled and they started walking in a half-squat through the meadow, holding their guns in front of them like the plastic soldiers we played with.

We'd seen all the stickered cars parked in the driveway: *Get the US out of the UN and the UN out of the US. AuH2O. John Birch Society. Minutemen.*

A swishing in the grass and the mechanical creaking of katydids. Fireflies flaring. Now they were silhouettes, a darkness moving steadily toward us through high grass, rifles swaying, fingers curled around triggers.

ARRAN

You'll want to know what it means.
I cannot say—his one arm withered
in the womb, with the other he leaned
against the apple tree, beside starlings' feathers

and splashes of shit where once
were bluebirds, legend has it, flitting
brightly, warbling softly, flouncing
where now the stalwart stare, fittingly,

perhaps, sings like a rusting-out machine.
Twenty years since he by chance
caught me in that same tree he leaned
against and chased me till I wet my pants,

that rifle swinging madly in his good,
God-given, sinister hand, him
screaming that he'd kick my ass or shoot
me dead. We were Kennedy dems.

They were Birchers. We were Irish.
They were Scots. It all sounds so simple,
inevitable, our tensions, our skirmishes
with rocks and sticks, when, for example,

his boys, all five, assembled a "war party,"
and my brothers lined-up straight away
like some ancient battle of the foolhardy,
marching blind "like cattle o'er the lea."

We fought with sticks and stones
urged on by something in our blood,
or something someone said at home.
All so clear, those battles that we brewed.

But once, we crept up to their house.
His wife saw us, waved us in. Fed us
scones she'd baked, encouraged us to browse
the bins of oats and spices, led us

to her pantry, gave us bags of fenugreek
and sprouts. Who knew such kindness lay
within the fortress walls? We'd heard the squeak
and squeal before the younger Arran played

his sunset bagpipe tunes, and they'd stirred
some kinship that we'd find and lose again.
And loss was why we finally stood
Beside that tree and talked. His wife was gone,

his children, too, and though we thought
he hated us, and I guess he thought the same,
we were the last left standing. We'd fought,
though for what now we couldn't say,

and when we talked, we knew the names,
the stories, who'd lived where and when
and what had happened. The Zelensky girl, her shame
at getting pregnant; her hunchback friend.

My brother and I were shingling
the family house. Two whole weeks
he came and stood below us, bringing
scones and coffee, light and sweet.

Every day, with something on his mind—
though he never got the nerve to say
out loud what vexed him all this time.
We talked instead about the way

the trees had grown, the meadow changed,
the orchard finally gone to rot.
He'd ask us our dead brothers' names
and remember something he'd forgot—

wasn't Jim a bowler? Didn't Stephen ride?
Our mom, he'd say, was quite the dancer.
And then one day he didn't come—a Friday.
Sunday we learned he'd loaded up his camper,

drove to Sandpoint to meet his Bircher friends
and his bagpipe-playing, namesake son.
I pictured him then, bag of nails pinned
beneath his chin, elbow on a ladder rung,

standing on my mother's father's land,
face whitened by the morning sun,
handing up a shingle with that hand—
the dexterous and also sinister one.

FASHION REPORT

Was it a shirt in or a shirt out age? No one knew for certain. It was clearly not a rolled pants era, though a few, in isolated moments, mistook it for one. It was not a blue eye shadow and pink lipstick era, that seemed clear. White calf length boots? No. Arching eyebrows drawn severely on with a chunk of fire-hardened charcoal? Nyet. Was it a straight flat hair epoch? Or a soft fluffy curve around the edges of the face moment? Opinion on bangs or the vasty open sheen of the forehead was mixed. Even the experts seemed divided on whether it was the power stiletto or the innocent wonder of the flip-flop. Could the two exist side by side? Editorials in the major periodicals suggested this was unlikely. And the CPO, the Nehru, the various vestments of oligarchy? Consigned, it would seem, to the thrift shops, but beginning, again, a secret assault from those bunkers. Was this a sign of discomfort with the wars or an embrace of the ranks and charges therein? A secret army of ragtag missionaries from the marijuana growing loft-dwellers? Or simply a love of the smart epaulets, the slimming effect elicited by the clean lines of the militaristic? Such questions were remanded to the authorities for further study. Experts were quite sure it was not a loose open collar and thick silver chain era. Nor was it a button-down era, though some pressed for such a shift. It seemed that it was neither the wide tie and suspenders of rising markets nor a thin-tied rejection of traditional monetary policy. Glasses were incoherent, reflecting a certain befuddlement among the populace. Was it a subtly ambitious and slightly ironic wire-rimmed moment or did this age call for the thick black-rims of realpolitik? The electrical taped bridge of solidarity seemed entirely absent from the optic landscape. The recent outbreak of irony among T-shirt slogans introduced uncertainty into the market forecasts. Even the hairstyles, mixed as they were from buzzcut to bouffant, proved unreliable as indicators. At parties, the frisson of off-the-grid patchouli mixed easily with upwardly-mobile Chanel, scuttling all attempts to read consumer confidence. Were we approaching an age? Was the incoherence a sign? And why now this incoherence, this unseemly recklessness among the wearers of clothing? And why these snappy chapeaus, when all the experts had predicted bare heads and baseball caps? Where were our vestments taking us? What would be the human cost?

POPSTAR

The popstar has arrived. Her people have apparently rented and converted a ranch south of town to her specifications. Rumors of a lap pool and an exercise room, a home theater, have been authenticated by local craftsmen, some of whom claim to have seen the popstar through the tinted windows of her Humvee.

Already, the first tremors have been felt in the markets. Clearly, we have much to be thankful for. The wait staff has assembled at the door. A new optimism has filtered down from the management. Even now, the help is dust-bustering the windowsills and bedposts. Management has sent runners to the ranches and farms to gather meats and vegetables for the expected onslaught of dinner customers. News crews have decamped on the outskirts of town. They will also, it is thought, need to be provisioned.

The mayor has purchased a red Maserati with public monies. Though some were outraged, it has become clear that this is a necessary addition to the city's vehicular profile. In public pronouncements, he notes that we need to appear to be conversant with the current standards. It's true, with his new hand-tooled boots, his new suit, his new hat and bolo tie, he cuts an imposing figure. He is, as a recent *Journal* report suggests, avatar of a new dusty, though largely wrinkle-free, modernism. And he has stirred suddenly from his political lethargy. He has decreed a moratorium on autographs. New legislation on gawking is working its way through the House.

It is thought that the popstar has chosen our town to avoid the constant hectoring by the media in places like Paris and New York. It is thought that she will want to view our artworks, which have become important once again due to a recent reassessment by a leading east coast critic. It is thought that she will want to party with our bearded hipsters, our refugees from the de rigeur, who have achieved a greater hipness by avoiding the hip. This movement interests, sources say, the popstar. Her people believe the unhip hipster movement may have a long-term effect on the popstar market. Like our unhip hipsters, she is listening to The New Silence. She has collected all the central ensembles of the movement on the original vinyl. She is expected to Not Dance to The New Silence at the Roost. Observers say she is quite accomplished, conversant with all the non-moves of the new non-dance. It is thought that she will recruit several of our local non-dancers for her new non-dance troupe. Some suggest she, herself, has achieved moments of complete quiescence on the non-dance floor.

But all is not well. Dissenters believe she is exploiting us. They point to the technological resources she requires to buttress her legendary beauty. They note that she has brought a staff of outsiders to attend her hair, her nails, her lips and eyes. They claim to have intercepted a package filled with outsourced eyewear and bangles. *Isn't our fashion eyewear perfectly adequate?* They ask. *Are not our bangles among the finest in the area?* These dissenters have gathered in the center of town and are waving signs and shouting. In the interest of free speech, the mayor has built a small corral for dissent at the intersection of Main Street and Highway 90.

    Luckily, most of the citizenry is more concerned with the bigger questions: Is the popstar as hot, less hot, or hotter than she appears to be in her videos? Is that her real hair or an extension? Is her equally famous, fabulously wealthy husband also in town? And what does she think of us? Does she approve our new dance hall? The natural food store? The gazebo? Does she approve our austere and multiplicative art? Our vague new music? Will she have drinks with us at the Dustbin Bar? Some are hoping she will purchase a house and settle down and become one of us. For others, this is a terrifying idea. If she is one of us, she will stop being mysterious, they argue. Then what?

    The mayor has parked his Maserati at the entrance of our city. He is wearing his suit, his luxurious beaver-felt Stetson. In the distance, we can see the dust rising above a caravan of Hummers. We have all assumed our positions.

    Our world-renowned tuba ensemble has begun honking from the gazebo.

WISH FOR A YOUNG WIFE
after Theodore Roethke

You think things will get finally done but miss the point.
The point is that new tasks must be grown to fill each day.
While you prepare for eternity your papers and your poems,
she's planning for tomorrow and a holiday abroad,
scheduling tight and keeping neat the vestibule
where guests will stomp the age's weather from their boots.

Boots you thought were good enough to walk you to the car
prove doddering enough she's tossed them out. She's found
a pair so stylish they have no teeth for ice, no grit for snow,
and has sent you to the grocery in them. With a list of foods
that seem designed for birds or mice—some seeds, some sprouts,
some greens clearly slaughtered in their youth. The meat

is made from plants, which means you'll save the earth—
for someone younger, while the young save you for nothing
but the earth. And *in you'll go*, long before this wife,
this wispy wife who cycles through a virtual France
while she stacks her cash and posts her latest hiphop dance
to Instagram. Some wishes are like fish, too slick to grasp;

others are like wind, they fill the house, but once inside,
they're everywhere, and, also, sir, impossible to find.

PETTING ZOO, CERRILLOS, NEW MEXICO
after Richard Hugo

Lode the rains washed down from Golden
still floats the Galisteo's rush. But pans
don't flash with color here. The twelve hotels
have crumbled back to clay. The aging
hippie's livestock huddles at the gate;
his thin goats clamber on each other's back
to lip the feed the toddler reaches up.
His museum's filled with skins and gems,
pot-shards, tools nobody's ancestors carved
a living with, all washed by hopeful light.
No hope. The sun betrays its promise.
Weather so ideal it wears the mesas down.
Seeds stay dull. Flowers nod and swoon,
their beauty spent in a day, an afternoon.
One night, the local libertarian, a biker,
drunk, enraged, fired at the crowd outside
The Mineshaft Tavern. He wants that moment back.
The aging hippie tells the realtor his tenant
must be female, young and insouciant. His wife
just shifts her hips. A black goat nips
the bag of feed, knocks it from the toddler's hand.
She cries. A donkey brays. The world won't change.
Here's a home for misery, dull ache. Another
day away from 1828, when men cried "Gold!"
and led their mules into the hills. They named
their clump of shacks and tailings Golden–
the name meant heaven–but wound up
earthbound, picking at a seam of coal instead.

JANE SAYS

Jane says she's leaving Sergio in Boston and starting a new life in Providence.

Jane says Lacan is right: We're doomed to the arc of romantic love–the intense role-playing at the outset, the wonder at discovering our soul mate, followed by bitter disappointment.

Jane says she's chronic.

Jane says she loves the illusion, hates the reality.

Jane says this hangnail is driving her nuts.

Jane says Providence is beautiful this time of year—gray, rainy, cold.

Jane says punk is dead again.

Jane says punk likes being dead because then it can rise from the ashes again.

Jane says punk is dead when people thinks it's alive and alive when people think it's dead.

Jane says she's embarrassed by my car and I should sideswipe something quick so we can tape a black garbage bag over her window.

Jane says Napoleon was way cooler than people give him credit for. He was stylish in defeat. What more could you want in a man?

Jane says in two weeks her unemployment runs out and she'll probably have to sell her body.

Jane says I should get in on the sale early, before the diseases move in.

Jane says unless she can make the rent on what her parents send her.

Jane says she lived in Providence for three months in 2007, but left when her boyfriend signed a major label deal.

Jane says his punk band turned slick and she stopped trusting him.

Jane says CEOs are dyeing their hair purple now.

Jane says she's vegan *and* a vampire.

Jane says that's been difficult.

Jane says if you turn here, you come out by the Brown University bookstore.

Jane says there's a homeless guy with a boombox on this street who paints himself silver and thinks he can do the robot. It's pathetic and hilarious, we should stop.

Jane says it's a metaphor for love.

Jane says we should get together, we could skip straight to bitter disappointment. It'll be great.

Jane says we can start throwing things right away.

Jane says we can move out before we move in together.

Jane says it'll be groundbreaking.

Jane says she's not really going to trick herself out, it's just a ploy to extort rent money from her parents.

Jane says her parents live in Newport and they get squeamish when she moves to Providence.

Jane says all of her friends are trying to look like they're already dead.

Jane says if you drop me here, I'll hold that parking place for you and you can circle the block.

Jane slaps her black boots and says anybody trying to take the parking spot will get one of these up his ass.

Jane says okay it's your gas.

Jane says we could circle all day.

Jane says she did acid once and spent the night vomiting in a bathtub.

Jane says she drinks Laphroig out of a paper bag. Makes her feel bougie and righteous at the same time.

Jane says she's through with manarchy.

Jane says she's moving in with a chick and joining the new feminarchy movement.

Jane says of course you haven't heard of it, I just made it up.

Jane says life sucks and then you swim upstream to spawn.

Jane says thanks for the ride.

Jane says you're cute I wish you were twenty years younger.

Jane says could you spare a few bucks?

Jane says are you going to eat the other half of that Subway?

THEORETICALLY SPEAKING

Dearest Aimee,

Regarding my subject position as contextualized within our psychosexual relationship, I can finally acknowledge my own gynocentric obsessions, my heterosexism, the epistemic violence, the fissures, the transgressive, if ultimately heteronormative codes, by which our discourse achieved a kind of canonicity. My gaze, gendered and hegemonic as it was, marginalized your alterity, even as a certain *cri de coeur* authored and simultaneously demystified the master narrative of our sexual praxis. It is true I contextualized our pleasure from within the phallocentric; I realized too late that a strictly historicist view might have decentered the erotics of reified desire in which we were imprisoned. I will gladly relinquish *The History of Sexuality, volumes 1 & 2*, if you will convey to me at your earliest convenience my hardcover *Glas*.

    Yours,

    ~~Jean~~

MUSIC MEN

Chris Isaak arrives early in yellow swim trunks, a bright towel hanging like a horseshoe around his neck. He's been on the beach with two supermodels-in-training. They're with him now as he looks for a piano. Suddenly, a diaphanous song materializes above him. He whispers into its ear. It follows him into the studio, clacking on its oversized heels.

Van Morrison arrives late, coughing into his fist. He spent the night on Cypress Avenue. A pale woman in a large black hat, her thin arms festooned with bracelets, floats behind him. He needs a guitar right now. A song is pouring out of his chest. He catches it in the soundhole of the guitar.

Chris Isaak has his people call for an arugula salad, with cranberries and walnuts and thinly sliced Ahi, a bottle of champagne. He passes out chopsticks to the supermodels-in-training. They circle the salad as if it were an altar to loveliness and success. Chris Isaak lights a candle. They all laugh and eat. With chopsticks, Chris Isaak plucks an arugula leaf stuck to one woman's pouty lower lip.

Van Morrison becomes famished. He discovers a lamb in the meadow behind the studio. He slaughters it with a tenor saxophone. A single blow to the head. He butchers it, lays a fire using old Decca labels and peat, then roasts the lamb on a rock he sets in the middle of the fire. Lustily does he eat the lamb, slipping chunks also into the red mouth of his woman.

Chris Isaak has a pallet made on the floor. He puts a sleep mask on. The supermodels-in-training curl beside him. They lay their heads carefully on his chest, facing each other. Chris Isaak places his hands lightly on their heads, slipping his fingers into their hairstyles. They sleep.

Van Morrison must slumber. He flops on the floor. Pulls his woman down with him. Together, they kick at things—dishes, books, guitars, horn charts, discarded lyrics—until they've cleared enough space. Van Morrison pulls the small woman to his chest. Holds her tight until dawn.

Chris Isaak is feeling it and the musicians arrive. They uncase their instruments. Tune. Chris Isaak runs over the lyric. It's about two supermodels-in-training. Palm trees. Laughing and drinking champagne. During the bridge, they all roll in the wet sand. But one of the women has left Chris Isaak. The other won't tolerate his advances. He aches for one, longs for the other, talks to neither. O, sweet conundrum. His voice quavers with it. He's never been happier.

Van Morrison wants to record. He calls up a saxophonist, a drummer, and a bass player. The saxophonist's instrument has been run over by a truck. The drummer was recently blinded in a chemical spill. The bass player is homeless. Van counts it off, lays out the chords. "Hut," he shouts and the drummer whacks the tom. He's whispering where they thought he would sing, crooning where they thought he would growl, growling where they thought he'd call for a solo. The woman in the black hat is lost to swaying. She takes a long solo with her hips and shoulders. Outside the surviving lambs are bleating. The rain slaps the roof like a tambourine.

THE BILLVILLE ELECTROCUTION

Let us say it straight, right here, right now, at the outset: Only we natives of Billville know how to correctly dance the Billville Electrocution. While we acknowledge that some in our town are profiting from the burgeoning, cult-like interest in the Electrocution and the various pilgrimages to the corner of Main Street and Paseo Robles, where the dance was invented, we have, after a careful review of the extant YouTube videos, come to some alarming conclusions.

In these videos, we see groups of outlandishly dressed youths of many cultures—it has become a worldwide trend, indeed—in the sudden outbursts they call "Flash Mobs." And, certainly, they are having fun and entertaining each other with their strange, clownish attire and their oversized, brightly-colored sunglasses and wigs, and, while we are not opposed to either fun or entertainment, particularly in these depressed and possibly apocalyptic times, with each installment, each new clip posted, it becomes clearer and clearer: These dancers have not been properly instructed. Nor have they paid proper homage to the dance's origins. Their carefully choreographed arm movements, rampant smiles, rolling eyes, and sexually suggestive hip gyrations are simply not part of the Billville Electrocution. The Billville Electrocution requires dedication, study, and, we would suggest, genuine roots in the Billville community.

We do not come to this conclusion lightly. We have gone back to the original footage of Joe Bob Daniels on the fateful day when he inadvertently invented the dance across from Atkin's Hardware. When the lightning struck and he began spasming, our first thoughts were, of course, for his eventual wellbeing. But we also knew that we needed to continue to roll footage on Stu Atkins' helmet cam. We knew this would go viral. We knew Joe Bob's bad luck would be a boon for us all, and, indeed, that has been the case.

Those who wish to understand the Electrocution should look carefully at the sequence of spasmodic head and arm gestures that begin at 3:11 and continue undiminished, though subtly modulated, until 7:14. Here is the core, the heart, the pith and fiber of the Billville Electrocution.

Here we can see the unique cultural inheritance that Joe Bob brings to the dance. The entire history of Billville is reenacted: the long days of peace among the natives, the women gathering berries along the Billville River, the men spearing peccaries in the arroyo, the children being birthed in the encampment—all of this appears in the Electrocution as a kind of euphoric swooning from 1:11 to 3:11; then the coming of the Europeans, the days of slaughter signaled by the sudden and repeated hatcheting motions that begin without warning at 3:11; the wild spinning from 4:35 to 5:14

indicate the cattle swarming across the land, the land being fenced, the ranch houses built, the poplars rising around them; and, finally, the developers arriving from the East, the trains rattling into the station, the military base spreading its metal arms, embracing the town—all are dramatized in the brilliant two minutes of frantic clutching and gasping before the prostration and final collapse at 7:14.

Given the gravity of the Billville Electrocution. Given the graceful, if at times spasmodic, reinterpretation of history. Given the reverence, the rootedness, the deep cultural significance, it is hard to see how any reinterpretation, any sudden manifestation, planned or unplanned, of the Billville Electrocution can be anything other than parody. Although some of our more vocal critics have called for laws, bans, law suits, orders to cease and desist, it is our hope that those engaged in the Electrocution movement will, after careful introspection, cease of their own free will. Therefore, have we undertaken this program of education and public forums. Therefore, have we enlisted the Billville Electrocution Dance Troupe, a group of young people trained and led by Joe Bob Daniels himself, whose inadvertent twitching and sudden vocalizations are, we believe, more than symptoms of some deep rewiring caused by the lightning strike, more than a dance step, a fad, an exploitable notoriety, but a glimpse into the future, not only of Billville but of this occasionally murderous, yet magnificent and dance-crazed country.

CARNAL IN THE LAND OF BLOOD AND BEAUTY
for Grant Hayunga

To make of fur a furred thing. To make
of fur a doe who is surprised to be a doe
who walks upright in the blood and danger.
To make a wolf lunging over marbled snow,
a falcon among flowers, a hare
bemused by a raven's headstand.
To make not only the night branches,
but the quavering owl [not pictured].
One way is to make everything look
like everything else; the harder way
is to make everything look like itself
and more than itself. Golden,
the cloven field, and the live oaks
nostalgic in the winter of their intentions.
The pronghorn's gaze radiates a wary
equanimity amid the burgeoning. Meanwhile,
the somnambulist wanders the blue night,
crows rise on wings of black flame,
and the skies grow menacing, if by menace
we mean the trees' stark clarity against the bright
omen of cloud. *Omen*, we say, a sound
more lips than tongue—half *ominous*, half *amen*.

ABJECTION
    after the paintings of Dirk DeBruycker

This is the beginning and the end, alpha and omega, the blotted-out place.
Here where the icons once paraded their sentiments.
Bleeding now because they cannot stop changing.
Bleeding now because they have been canceled.

If truth : beauty as *lamb : slaughter.*
Not Morocco. That, too, blotted-out.
And Belgium. And Dirk DeBruycker.
And the author of these words.

Canceled.
Now we are figures in paper.
What we intended, gone.
Into filigree, tracery, into splatter and wash.

All the lines uncleated.
Now we mean *So much is lost.*
Now we mean *Can you hear us at all.*
Now we mean *What beautiful obliteration.*

Someone said *Help me climb over this barbed cancellation.*
Past these creatures gnawing at absence.
Someone said *Why such whimsy in the face of—*
Someone said *And all of it canceled.*

Canceled: The body, impaled and lifted above the marketplace.
Canceled: The body sprawled across the spikes.
Canceled: The fruits and vegetables uncrated, the lamb carcasses splayed.
All of it painted in another language.

The absence calling us to another language.
The absence which has become the darkness.
The darkness where the meanings once slept, tails curled, heads on their paws.
The bodies stacked and covered with canvas.

The babies who would not last the night without their mothers
(who had died of cholera) lain gently in the back of a truck to die.
Fifty infants. Smooth, babyfat hands closing on nothing.
Hungry, but not afraid of cancellation.

We were eating popcorn when we noticed that the truck bed–
in the repetition, in the contrast of rough cloth and smooth faces–
was achieving a kind of formal elegance.
Then a darkness canceled all of it.

A canvas flap pulled down for protection, for privacy.
An artist's brush.
There were six paintings on the wall.
I wanted to crawl into the one whose center was obliterated.

Into the O of orgasm.
Into the birth canal.
Into the crown of thorns.
Into the zero.

THE FAILED SPRING

Barring a second assault, all should be well.
The current proprietor of the bird house
has launched an encomium of sorts from the acacia
lamenting the previous owner's poorly-made nest
and unhatched eggs, assuring us the new nest,
built directly on the first, entombing thereby
the earlier clutch of speckled eggs, is timed
to coincide with the end of the surprising
cold snap, the unforeseen winds from the east.
That we have chosen to call the group of eggs
a clutch. That the brittle remnants
of the oak's leaves, singed by frost, are being replaced
by tiny replicas sprouting like the hands
of the thalidomide boy you once watched
bowling with his feet. And how we love this
chance at recovery, this *overcoming*, this *triumph
of the spirit*, this . . . what? We know there's a word
for it, or many, in many languages, if we could
only recall them as the fulsomeness regathers
and sweeps over us like a Waikiki wave
or like a memory of other springs. Certainly
these vicissitudes mock our fatuousness, ask us
gently to get down from our high horses.
But whose horses are these? And when did
we mount them? It seems we woke here
already athwart these geldings and mares,
certain that spring would arrive with its lilacs
and birdsong, its vague promise to melt like a bonbon
in the mouth of summer, then disappear
into roguish fall and raffish winter, only to return
with its rains and sudden smells of wet soil,
warblers teetering in the elms, at least so far,
though it is early in this callous
and retributional century.

MANATEES

Manatees lounging in their underwater parlors,
drifting through the long afternoons like women
in an impressionist painting—given a Sunday, given
flowers and a rowboat, tea and lace. Manatees
in their rough hides, floating slowly over the weedbeds—
like women in the park. Or like dirigibles
in photographs, drifting through a black and white sky,
drifting toward the inevitable lashing and tethering,
one century giving way to the next, drifting
made obsolete by the churning engines, the props
turning to turbines, the quickening also in the pulse,
in the body's core, in the implicate order,
the human minds ticking in the shadows,
calculating, monitoring, the calculus of ardor
and need unscrolling into a world torqued by greed,
by cigarette boats cutting furrows in the shallows,
churning back to port, strafing the dreamy manatees,
the driver shaking his glass to cool the scotch,
the bikinied women, lovely now, lying on the deck,
lounging, turning brown and browner in the pitiless sun.

APOCALYPSE

Nobody was happy with the apocalypse. For some it lacked drama. Many had hoped for a series of explosions, bands of bulked-up, tattooed men riding atop mongrel machinery, hair blowing in the apocalyptic wind. Others hoped for lost tribes scrabbling across the windswept ghost cities, battling with remnant weapons for the small caches of unspoiled food that remained. Still others had hoped for clashes between superpowers featuring Blackhawks and stealth bombers, lasers fired from remote-controlled satellites. For some, the lack of a moral proved disturbing. Where was the righteousness we'd expected? Why hadn't the virtuous been sorted from the sinful? Where was the complex system of rewards and punishments we'd embraced? The randomness of the apocalypse was a topic that confounded many of the apocalypticians. Nobody had foreseen the long, slow, boring demise. Entropy and ennui, it seems, had few supporters. Nobody had predicted that the apocalypse would be marked by resignation and waiting, that the apocalypse would be more of a terminal diagnosis than a series of heroic interventions. Of course, there was drama when we understood it was over. When the measurements were taken. When the scientists appeared alongside the presidents and prime ministers and religious leaders. When they made the grim pronouncement. When the game was called because of darkness. Many of us gathered briefly in the streets to take action, but no action could be agreed upon. The wealthy and powerful had caches of food and drinking water. We knew they'd outlive us by days, months, maybe years, but most agreed this was no advantage. The scientists had run out of tricks. The food supply was dwindling. There was no clean water. The shift to solar energy made for an unending source of power, especially as the ozone layer thinned and disappeared, so most decided to go inside and play video games or watch television and movies, search the web for music videos, or videos of someone doing something incredibly stupid on a skateboard. Facebook became painful as lethargy and death made for a scroll of loss. Messages from afteriamgone.com started being forwarded in huge numbers. Letters from the dead pouring into the mailboxes of the living. Occasionally gunfire would erupt on the streets and people would mute their televisions and listen wistfully until the gunfire ceased. When the end came, we lifted our heads and nodded. The computers and videos went on without us, the animated characters dying and restarting, dying and restarting, the jingles floating out over the otherwise silent streets.

THE ROOM

In the beginning was a room,
a kind of ephemeral lodge
that enveloped us everywhere, held us
on the hillside overlooking the village,
along the river, in the alleys
of the contagious city. The room
was everywhere because it was built
of the shivering light on water,
the lightning crackle,
the *churr* of frog song at dusk.

Everything became part of the room—
the three gunshots in the otherwise
calm dawn, the slam and crunch
of metal, even the child
struggling to breathe in fever's grip.
The room held it all. *Come in
storm*, it said, *come in sunlight
and shadow, come in fistful of dollars,
palmful of coins, flood and fire,
sad party, door slam, ruined anniversary.*

But soon the room's walls,
always porous, began to dissipate.
The room stopped being a room.
It became a world just like the world.
So much inside that there was no place
for us. I woke this morning
thinking the room had been a dream,
but the room was real.
Where had it gone? How
could we get back in?

That room where everything
we touched was welcomed,
where even pain, when it entered,
bared its teeth and hissed,
then curled in the corner
and slept quietly, waking only
to take food from our hands,

making us, not happy, exactly, but alert,
our eyes full of sunlight and flax,
our ears tuned to birdsong and breeze.

VINTAGE

The singer sang a cappella for thirty seconds, then the beat dropped.
Now where were we? We kept talking about that cute thing
our granddaughter did. The kids wanted to talk about the failure
of cryptocurrency to capture the public's imagination.
Then we remembered the "kids" were thirty-something. The actual
kids were speaking a language we didn't recognize at all. We were
binge-watching our days and they were terrifying—pandemics,
deaths by cancer, inexplicable deaths, deaths of birds trembling
beside the plate glass. We kept voting for the least-offensive politician.
But we were governed by a shrill posse from up near the tree-line.
It was spring, and the finches were copulating in the peach tree
but it didn't cheer us. The skunks ambled through the arugula
like mental patients. We couldn't remember the name
of that disease that kept you from remembering. We couldn't
remember the name of the person we could call who would know.
We were googling it, typing into our phones with a single
shaking finger. Looking over then through our glasses.
All the knowledge we had acquired no longer applied—
the past tense of *lie*, where the semi-colon went, the past tense
of *lead*, how to calculate fractions, the capital of Idaho.
How had we been so wrong about the future? No jet packs
but all these algorithms. Everything extruded. Everything we loved
now vintage. Yet still, in isolated pockets, people were making music
on actual instruments. Still, in isolated pockets, actual food from gardens.
In the swamps, actual frogs, harrumphing in the cattails,
redwings trilling and spreading their wings, a lone heron
drifting ghostly above its ghostlier reflection, and somebody's
granddaughter hunkered in the mud, saying "wait," saying "frogs,"
just crouched and still, just listening to our vintage world.

ODE TO THE CORONAVIRUS

Teach me how to love the cough, the test,
the social distance, canceled prom, empty gym,

the steady slide into impoverishment.
My ears, at this late age, make of silence

a steady hiss, so I'm never alone, except
with my failures. Failure to forget myself

completely for just a moment. Even as
my granddaughter swings her tiny foot—*golpe,*

golpe, golpe—I'm thinking *my* granddaughter, as if
the reckless joy she brings to the dance

is part mine. But nothing is mine. And that's
the lesson you came to teach. Everything

crumbling. Everything suspended a moment
like pollen on the water at the top of a waterfall.

Or like a stray dog in traffic, lunging & turning.
Or a bat in the bedroom flapping raggedly

toward one wall & the next. If just for one
moment I could still the hiss in my ears,

the shuddering in my chest, or call it
something else—a *shimmering*—then would I be

like the humming stones at the waterfall's foot
that welcome the weight of water & pollen:

golpe fuerte, golpe de suerte, golpe mortal.

ABOVE THE BEJEWELED CITY

I was a guest in their house. A house
set at the lit edge of a great city. Below us
a virus was floating like dust motes
through the streets. Their daughter
had raised a jarful of butterflies—
not a jar exactly, more like a vase.
I was having drinks with them in violation
of the latest edicts from the premier.
When they weren't speaking to me
they spoke a bright guttural language
like the one you might imagine
river rocks would speak
at the bottom of a mountain stream.
At one point in the evening,
the daughter rose politely from her chair
and performed a kind of flamenco,
snaking her hands into the air as if
pulling herself through dense undergrowth.
How can I explain? The world was ending.
In the city below people were collapsing,
struggling to breathe. I didn't know why
there were fires or why smoke
marbled the sky above the buildings.
I tried to imagine individual deaths,
eyes looking out from behind glass visors,
hands reaching up to be held.
It seemed the least I could do.
We moved onto the balcony
that overlooked the city.
We brought the vase of butterflies.
Flashing red lights jeweled the streets below us.
Sirens flared and stopped and flared again.
We stood quietly in the darkness.
As I understood it, my host was
a professor of some rarely spoken language.
His wife sang cabaret songs in a local bistro.
We removed the cover of the vase
and released the butterflies.
Would you believe me if I told you

that they sprang from the jar as though
forced upward by a burst of air, and
that they did not flutter away into the night
but one by one landed on that girl
until she was covered with wings,
all gently pulsing? Oh, readers,
it was lovely there on that balcony
above the dying world. And for a moment,
I thought she might step away
and leave the butterflies hanging there
in the shape of a girl.
After a while she pointed to herself.
What's happening? she whispered.
Her parents said something
in their underwater language
that caused her to begin slowly turning,
and the butterflies began to loosen their grip
and flutter into the night,
catching the light a moment
before they were lost in the general darkness.
*That is how it has always been done
in our country*, my host told me.
With one such as her.
And I believed him, dear reader.
Wouldn't you have? On such a night,
in such a world—

THE CITY OF NEW ORLEANS

*"Through the Mississippi darkness,
rolling down to the sea."*
—Steve Goodman

1. Riding

                I was half-sleeping
        in my seat when I woke and noticed that Gregory,
    who is autistic and a little unpredictable,
was not in his seat. I thought I'd better find him,
  so rose and skinnied past the sleepers.
I heard him talking softly in the next car
and sat where he wouldn't see me.
      The men were not, as the song has it, "dealing cards
        in the club car." Instead, my stepson
            was telling intricate stories about his work
            in pediatric intensive care
        at the University of New Mexico, with such
    brutal authority that the men
  probably believed him. He detailed
the terrible emergencies he'd had to attend—
the burns, broken backs, brain tumors—
  and the distraught parents he'd had to console.
    When it was over
        the men thanked him for his service,
            then wandered back to their seats to encourage
              a couple hours of sleep before dawn
            and what would be, for them, just the ordinary
        sweat and labor of a New Orleans day,
    though we would see a 6'3" woman,
  naked from the waist up, stride
through the Quarter, watch hundreds
of disheveled Santas weaving the streets,
      and witness Gregory mounting the trolley steps
        alone to ride toward whatever imaginary or real
           adventures awaited him, which made me think—
          in a quick panicked flash—*how
      would we ever know?* And then
    the trolley was gone,
  rumbling and scraping, rocking
toward the next improbable stop.

2. Operating

That's what I wrote, but I skipped over the amazement I'd felt listening to Gregory talk. He'd spent his life in hospitals and had heard hundreds of stories. But I'd never heard him make that leap into someone else's skin. He slipped so easily from patient to doctor. He had no fear of being discovered. If someone challenged him, he doubled down: "The girl had a brain tumor *and* was burned over 60% of her body *and* had leukemia." "That's awful," one guy said, probably the drunkest of them from the way he lifted his head as if a heavy weight were hanging from his neck. "Just awful." "How did her parents bear it?" another man said. "I had to fire all the nurses in the department," Gregory said. "They kept calling in sick. There was so much work." "Of course, you did," a younger man on the periphery chimed in. "You had to." He told about the day he met the helicopter himself. A girl maybe seven or eight, broken legs, broken arm, fractured skull, blood everywhere. "And not a reliable nurse in sight." He operated by himself that day. It took him six hours, but she lived. "Great work, man," the young guy said. "Important work." And Gregory kept going like that for an hour while I sat in the back, pretending to read. Maybe I should have scolded him. Maybe I should have told the men that nothing he said was true. But why? Once we'd caught him lying and asked him why he'd done it. "I just want to be someone," he'd said, "with interesting stories to tell."

3. Waiting

And there's this. In Chicago, while we waited for the train, we walked to a small windy beach tucked behind the high-rises. It was my favorite part of the trip and I can't say why. We sat in the sand to escape the breeze and look out at Lake Michigan. A few ducks dipped their heads, *tippling*, I want to call it—though that's the wrong word—in the shallows. The lake seemed like an ocean. We were about to go on a great adventure. Everything seemed possible. And the sand and the breeze and the sun. I can't tell you. Gregory and Teresa. Me. The three of us. Just waiting. Maybe that was it. Maybe I was wrong about waiting. Maybe waiting is the best part. Nothing to do for an hour, the sun shining. The lake. The water going out. The same water coming back in.

THE FAMOUS POET
for Izzy

The family dog has escaped! Now even the famous poet must throw on his ratty sweatshirt and boots. Even the famous poet must find the keys that are probably in the pants he wore yesterday, that are probably in the washer. Even the famous poet must decide to walk the dark streets instead. He must trip over the skateboard in the middle of the walk. He must think, Who left a skateboard in the middle of the walk? Who made it dark out here? What sort of god engineers a big bang, a ball of gases, some carbon and oxygen, a spark of life, a one-celled organism, then two, some water, some plants, a swimming creature that crawls onto the mud flats, amphibians, reptiles, birds, mammals, primates, australopithecus, neanderthal, homo sapiens, a stone age, an iron age, some dark ages, a renaissance, a skateboard, a punk in a beanie, a kick flip and a careless rush to dinner, an escaped dog, a brisk walk, a dark night, a poet? What sort of god lets the dog bolt between the screen door and the jamb and rush towards the street? And just when the famous poet had sat down to compose a sonnet! A sonnet about tennis and how tennis is so much like life—the serve, the follow-through, the return, the volley, even the net, yes, so much is about the net! The famous poet wanders through the neighborhood. He shines his famous flashlight into the shrubbery, behind the shrubbery, under the shrubbery. What sort of dog heads for the shrubbery? Surely there are loose dogs in the alleys? Surely there is some stinky trouble to get into? The poet remembers stinky trouble fondly. Surely there is a villanelle about stinky trouble awaiting him. But where is that dog? The famous poet never liked that dog. He secretly thought the dog would kill him while his wife and children slept. A quick nip to the jugular, and he'd have to forego the great poems of his later years. He flicks off the flashlight. Better, the famous poet thinks, that the dog wanders into the highway. The world needs the famous poet's later work. The ponderous poems of failure and death. The world doesn't need a rottweiler-chow mix who doesn't sit or lie down or roll over or come when he's called. They need a sestina about that dog! Yes, even the children would prefer a sestina, though they think they want to throw a frisbee and cuddle the dog, put ribbons in his fur at Easter and Christmas. But a sestina! The famous poet begins thinking of seven good words. Maybe *collar* because it can be used as verb or noun or even an adjective. Which reminds him of the Eurasian collared doves in the back yard and how all day they coo *kangaroo stew kangaroo stew* and the dog charges at them and they flap ponderously just out of his reach. The worthless dog! The famous poet watches the night stars for a few minutes thinking about death and despair, then turns towards home. When he gets to the back door the dog is there, terrified, throwing his body at the screen door over and over, scratching, whimpering, and the poet thinks, *me too, buddy, me too*, and he throws himself at the screen and rips through to the other side and they tumble and skid together across the slippery floors looking for the humans—where are the humans?—shivering and whining and rushing down the halls, looking for the warm bodies that they find gathered by the television, and they throw themselves on them, their hearts hammering in their chests. They bury their faces in laps and hands and armpits and hair, howling and quivering, cooing and yelping, all of them, body to body to body in the flickering dark.

A STRUCTURE FOR OUR GRIEF

Build it of plastic that lasts a million years but quickly comes unhinged and unglued and gets left at the curb to be lifted onto a truck by mechanical arms and taken to the landfill, where it gradually decays into flakes and chunks, some of which are eaten by gulls and terns, who fly off to the ocean and shit while they paddle the waves until a whale comes seining and swallows that plastic along with all the other plastic—the bottles and cheap sunglasses, the ghostly bags—and its digestive system clogs and fails and the whale, starving, begins thrashing and groaning, and the other whales gather and try to comfort it while it founders and dies and floats to the ocean's surface where birds and fish feed on its carcass and the waves eventually push it gently onto a beach where the sunbathers and swimmers find it, gathering around to look at the hole where the eye was, the half skeleton half flesh of the fluke, until they can't stand the stench and head back to their blankets and coolers and sunscreen, while the other whales drift in the distance, rising to blow and diving back to the depths to mourn, sounding their squeaks and clicks, deep hums and squeals that can be heard, scientists say, by other whales four thousand miles away.

ASTERISK AS ORNAMENT

Indicating neither *grave* nor *allegro*
and sounding, on the inner ear,
like a madrigal of zithers. A madrigal,
by which I mean a pale origin, a stasis

among the statuary, a blankness given
shape, a diminutive star. O Aristarchus
of Samothrace, when you leaned
through candlelight, scattering stars

upon the text, you marked each absence
or untranslatable clause, each star-
crossed transit from crucible to crux,
as if absence were itself a passage.

Jon Davis is the author of five chapbooks and seven full-length poetry collections, including, most recently, *Above the Bejeweled City* (Grid Books, 2021). He has received a Lannan Literary Award, the Lavan Prize from the Academy of American Poets, and two National Endowment for the Arts Fellowships. His poems have appeared in numerous anthologies, including *Four Quartets: Poetry in the Pandemic; Photographers, Writers, and the American Scene; Poet's Choice; Sixty Years of American Poetry; The Best of the Prose Poem; No Boundaries: Prose Poems by 24 American Poets*; and *Telling Stories: A Writer's Anthology*. His poems have been translated into Spanish, Arabic, KiSwahili, and Vietnamese. He taught creative writing and literature for thirty years, twenty-eight of them at the Institute of American Indian Arts. In 2013, he founded the Low Residency MFA in Creative Writing at IAIA, which he directed until his retirement in 2018. He served as the City of Santa Fe's fourth poet laureate. He currently teaches poetry and fiction online and can be found at jondavispoet.com.

www.ingramcontent.com/pod-product-compliance
Lightning Source LLC
LaVergne TN
LVHW041552070426
835507LV00011B/1057